BLACK WIDOWS

Blaine Wiseman

SPIDERS

www.av2books.com

Step 1
Go to **www.av2books.com**

Step 2
Enter this unique code

QVJRUBGCI

Step 3
Explore your interactive eBook!

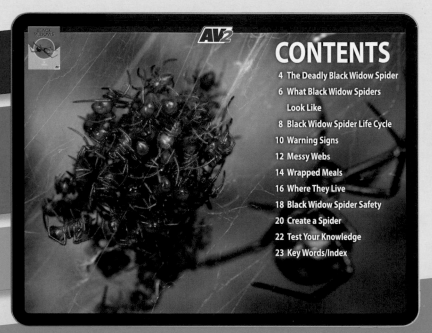

CONTENTS
4 The Deadly Black Widow Spider
6 What Black Widow Spiders Look Like
8 Black Widow Spider Life Cycle
10 Warning Signs
12 Messy Webs
14 Wrapped Meals
16 Where They Live
18 Black Widow Spider Safety
20 Create a Spider
22 Test Your Knowledge
23 Key Words/Index

AV2 is optimized for use on any device

Your interactive eBook comes with...

Contents
Browse a live contents page to easily navigate through resources

Audio
Listen to sections of the book read aloud

Videos
Watch informative video clips

Weblinks
Gain additional information for research

Try This!
Complete activities and hands-on experiments

Key Words
Study vocabulary, and complete a matching word activity

Quizzes
Test your knowledge

Slideshows
View images and captions

... and much, much more!

SPIDERS
BLACK WIDOWS

Contents

2 AV2 Book Code
4 The Deadly Black Widow Spider
6 What Black Widow Spiders Look Like
8 Black Widow Spider Life Cycle
10 Warning Signs
12 Messy Webs
14 Wrapped Meals
16 Where They Live
18 Black Widow Spider Safety
20 Create a Spider
22 Test Your Knowledge
23 Key Words/Index

Introduction

The Deadly Black Widow Spider

Black widow spiders are the best-known **widow** spiders. Widow spiders have sharp fangs with powerful **venom**. This protects them from **predators**. It also helps them hunt their **prey**. They use their long legs and strong bodies to climb and build webs.

Black widow webs are made from very strong silk. It is being studied to create new materials for humans to use.

Parts
of a
Spider

Eyes

Pedipalps

Fangs

Legs

Spinnerets

What Black Widow Spiders Look Like

Black widow spiders have large, round **abdomens** and eight long legs. Males and females look very different.

Females are about twice as big as males. They have shiny black bodies with red or orange markings. Male black widows are usually a light brown color. They may have red and white stripes along their sides.

A female black widow
spider can be
1.5 inches
(3.8 centimeters) long.

There are
5 types of
widow spiders in the
United States.

Black Widow Spider Life Cycle

Female black widow spiders live for up to three years. Males only live for one to two months. Female black widows may eat their **mates**. This is why they are called widows.

A female black widow can lay 900 eggs at one time. She wraps them in a **cocoon** and hangs it from her web. The eggs hatch about 30 days later. Baby black widow spiders may eat each other. Only a few become adults.

Sizing It Up

Zebra Jumping Spider
Leg Span: 0.3 inches (0.8 cm)

Western Black Widow Spider
Leg Span: 1.5 inches (3.8 cm)

Carolina Wolf Spider
Leg Span: 3 inches (7.6 cm)

Giant Golden Orb Weaver
Leg Span: 5.9 inches (15 cm)

Giant Huntsman Spider
Leg Span: 12 inches (30.5 cm)

Goliath Birdeater
Leg Span: 12 inches (30.5 cm)

Warning Signs

Black widows are known for their bright hourglass-shaped markings. Other **species** of widow spiders have different markings. These markings let large animals know that widow spiders are dangerous. They help keep the spider safe.

However, insects that widow spiders eat do not see these markings well. This lets widow spiders hide from their food.

More than **99 percent** of people bitten by black widows **survive**.

A black widow's venom is **fifteen times** more powerful than a rattlesnake's.

Messy Webs

Black widow spiders build webs close to the ground. A black widow's web may seem messy. It has long threads of silk hanging from a tangled area.

The spider builds its web this way for a reason. The tangled part traps flying insects and gives the spider **shelter**. The hanging threads are traps for crawling insects.

Spot the messy threads!

Wrapped Meals

When insects touch black widow webs, they become stuck. The black widow wraps the trapped prey in more silk, like a mummy.

A black widow bites its prey. This fills the prey with **chemicals**. The chemicals turn the spider's food into **liquid**. This makes it easier for the spider to eat.

Map

Where They Live

Widow spiders are found all over the world. The southern black widow is the most common in North America. It is found in every U.S. state except Alaska. Black widow spiders live in dark, dry areas. They are found in barns, basements, and hollow tree stumps.

Widow Spiders around the World

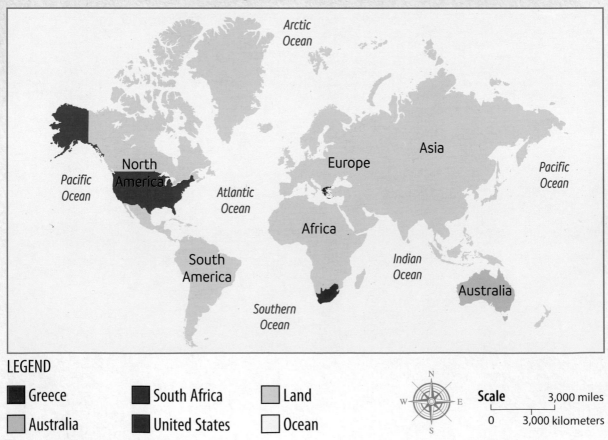

LEGEND

- ◼ Greece
- ◼ Australia
- ◼ South Africa
- ◼ United States
- ◻ Land
- ◻ Ocean

Scale

0   3,000 miles / 3,000 kilometers

Brown Widow Spider

Brown widow spiders come from African countries such as South Africa. There, they are known as brown button spiders. These spiders can also be found in North and South America, Australia, and Asia.

South Africa

United States

Western Black Widow

The western black widow spider lives in the western and southern parts of the United States. It can be found in deserts in the American Southwest.

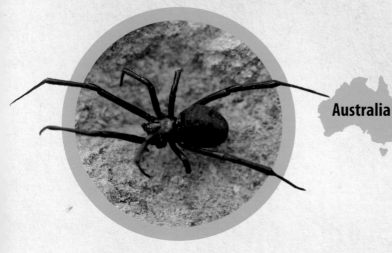

Australia

Redback Spider

Redback spiders are widow spiders from Australia. They bite about 2,000 people every year.

Greece

European Black Widow Spider

The European widow is found in the **Mediterranean**, in countries such as Greece. It has 13 red, yellow, or orange spots on its abdomen.

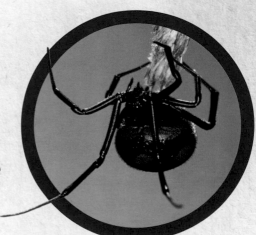

Black Widow Spider Safety

Black widow spiders usually only bite if they are disturbed. Children should never try to touch or move one.

Black widow spiders are the most venomous spiders in North America. Their bite is very painful. It can cause swelling, muscle aches, **nausea**, and trouble breathing. People who are bitten should see a doctor right away for **antivenom**.

Activity
Create a Spider

There are many different kinds of spiders in the world. They all have certain features in common. However, each spider also has its own features. They help the spider live in its home.

Make your own spider by answering the following questions:

1. What is your spider called?
2. Where does it live?
3. What features does it share with other spiders?
4. What features help it live in its home? How do these features do this?
5. What does your spider look like?
6. Use pencils, markers, or crayons to draw your spider living in its home. Make sure to include all of its features.

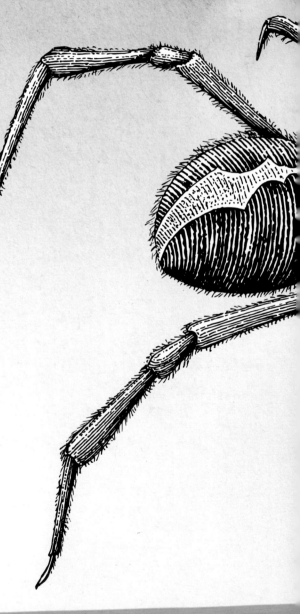

Test Your Knowledge

1
What shape is the marking on a black widow spider?

2
Do male and female black widow spiders look the same?

3
How many types of widow spiders are found in the United States?

4
How many eggs can a black widow spider lay at one time?

5
Do black widow spiders use webs to hunt?

6
What is the most common widow spider in North America?

7
Which spider is also called a brown button spider?

8
Which U.S. state does not have southern black widow spiders?

ANSWERS 1 Hourglass **2** No **3** 5 **4** 900 **5** Yes **6** Western black widow **7** Brown widow spider **8** Alaska

Key Words

abdomens: the back parts of spiders

antivenom: medicine that stops venom from working

chemicals: materials such as acid that cause things to change

cocoon: a sac that an animal makes using silk

liquid: material with no shape that flows like water

mates: members of a pair of animals that can reproduce, or have children

Mediterranean: the area around the Mediterranean Sea

nausea: sickness that includes feeling dizzy or light-headed

predators: animals that hunt other animals

prey: animals that are hunted by other animals

shelter: a safe space or home

species : a group of closely related animals or plants

venom: a toxic chemical produced by some animals

widow: a female whose mate has died

Index

antivenom 18
Australia 16, 17

bites 11, 14, 17, 18
brown widow 17, 22

European black
  widow 17

Greece 16, 17

redback spider 17

silk 4, 12, 14
South Africa 16, 17
southern black
  widow 16

United States 7, 16, 17, 22

venom 4, 11, 18

webs 4, 8, 12, 14, 22
western black widow 9,
  17, 22

Get the best of both worlds.

AV2 bridges the gap between print and digital.

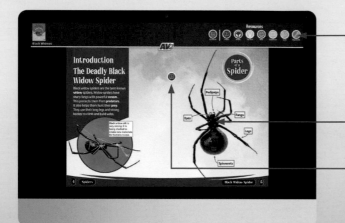

The expandable resources toolbar enables quick access to content including **videos**, **audio**, **activities**, **weblinks**, **slideshows**, **quizzes**, and **key words**.

Animated videos make static images come alive.

Resource icons on each page help readers to further **explore key concepts**.

Published by AV2
14 Penn Plaza, 9th Floor New York, NY 10122
Website: www.av2books.com

Library of Congress Control Number: 2019957549

ISBN 978-1-7911-2292-8 (hardcover)
ISBN 978-1-7911-2293-5 (softcover)
ISBN 978-1-7911-2294-2 (multi-user eBook)
ISBN 978-1-7911-2295-9 (single-user eBook)

Printed in Guangzhou, China
1 2 3 4 5 6 7 8 9 0   24 23 22 21 20

052020
101119

Designer: Terry Paulhus Project Coordinator: John Willis